CITIZEN

Jeff Weddle

Unlikely Books
www.UnlikelyStories.org
New Orleans, Louisiana

Unlikely Books
www.UnlikelyStories.org
New Orleans, Louisiana

CITIZEN RELENT

Always for Jill

The Order in Which They Appear

THREE
Hush, Little Baby 13
The Luck 14
Fire or Ice 15
Blessed Land 16
Responsibility of Eggnog 17
Perfecto 18
Nothing So Real 19
An Archeology 20
Maybe So 22
Decrepit 23
Always 24
In the End 25
No Heart Known or Needed 26
Please Pay Attention 27
What Love Does 30
Little Man 31
The Death We Deserve 32

TWO
#NeverAgain 35
What We Allow 36
This Is What You Do 37
Charlottesville 38
Therefore 39
American Dream 40
Yesterday in Heaven 42
America Was Great, I Guess, When 44
MAGA 45
Evangelical 47
Oh, Beautiful 48

Ain't that America? 49
Twilight of Empire 50
What We Now Endure 54
Holy Hell 56
Just Saying 57
Revelation 60
Beast 61
Your Turn 63
The American Way 64
You Know there Are Places Like That 65
May 4 67
Quiet Jim 69
Something You Should Know 71
Believe It 72
In Dubious Battle 73
In Our Time 74
New Testament 75
One Who Came Before 76
Naps Are the Best 77
This Is the Truth 78
The Circle Is Not Jealous of the Sphere 79

ONE

Prophesy Some 83
My Baby Wrote Me a Letter 84
Annelise Sometime 85
The Deadliest Man Alive 86
When We Left that Day 88
Sanctuaries 89
Caught 90
Something Like Love 91
Sweet Life 92
Red Flowers 93
Repitition of Saturday Night 94

Eternal   95
These Are the Things We Cannot Bear   96
Hello, It's Me   97
Buttercup and T-Bone   98
On Any Quiet Street   99
Those Were the Days   100
Heartbeat   101
Nighthawks   102
Reading *Pomes All Sizes*   104
Prestonsburg and All of It   105
Fun in the Sun   107
Floyd County   108

About the Author   111
Other Books by Jeff Weddle   112
Recent Titles from Unlikely Books   113

THREE

Hush, Little Baby

It ends, as important stories do,
with a woman nursing a child,
the morning bright and wafting
through an east-facing window,
framed in loving white
on the delicate breeze
of an April day.
The woman nurses through pain,
the child greedy
and incapable of gratitude.
She is well past thirty,
an inopportune age for nursing,
and she is tired,
and the baby will show
none of its gifts for many years,
and when, finally, the world
cries out the name she has given it,
she will be gone,
but that is a beginning,
and this is a story finished
on a beautiful morning
of birdsong and blood,
hours after a newly waning moon
gave up, unnoticed by the stars,
and, for all its beauty, died.

The Luck

your moment and mine
touch by chance
and we cannot bear
the empty spaces
of after and before
this embrace
is dancing with smoke
as we hold tight
and pretend
we are other
than deluded
that we are
more than dust
terrified and alone

Fire or Ice

My daughter, nine,
asked who would win
fire or ice
and I thought
for a second
about long term
verses right away
and I thought of
how to explain heat
and evaporation
and oxygen burn
and deprivation
and glaciers
and conflagration
and the power of opposites
and the unity of all things
and then I said ice
and she said okay
and everyone
was happy

Blessed Land

Someday I will go to Spain.
You must understand
that Spain is a metaphor for death
but that does not diminish its beauty.

Someday I will go there
and the colors will be bright
beneath the golden sun.
The bulls of Spain will be proud.
The bulls of Spain will be strong
and I will run among them,
proud and strong as any bull.
Someday I will go to Spain
by which I mean someday I will die.
It will be fine. Spain is the last
of the blessed lands. A gift.

Responsibility of Eggnog

She still asks and I usually say yes
just now it was eggnog
and yesterday
she wanted to bake a cake from scratch,
the frosting, too,
which we did from cobbled recipes
and conjured the best red velvet
that could happen
and the frosting, against all odds,
was delicious
but just now it was eggnog
and my young baker
required I pour her drink
because that is still, for now, my job
and too soon she will forget to ask,
a slight so easy to miss—
the responsibility of eggnog
glittering small
is gold and quickly spent

Perfecto

Smoke hangs solid
on fingers
like skin burns
inside chaos
like grandmother's
living room sheers
blowing a Sunday afternoon
behind the divan
hiding wasps
sexy in glass prison

Nothing So Real

Nothing so real as cigar ash
broken into beer can
a bit of backwash left
but nothing really wasted

An Archeology

It is the way the cutting is done
just-so angles
which are only haphazard
to the man with the knife
and a thousand thousand years
will pass
before the artifact is found
a few feet beneath
the surface of what was once
a manicured lawn
behind a small house
in an immaculate suburb
of a dead city
on a forgotten world
and the man
will not even be a memory
nor his kind
nor the gods he worshiped
and the thing
pulled by strange hands
from its hidden grave
will live again
in the histories written
by these strangers
and the meaning of the patterns
rendered by the slashing blade
will remain a delicious speculation

until the last light
of the last dying star
fades into darkness
and all is lost
forever

Maybe So

What if hell is a small dark room
a little too cold
with no chair
a window
you don't dare notice
and odd noises
every now and then
forever?

What if hell
is broken wind chimes
and old photographs
of people you have wronged
or else of those you have loved
who did not love you back?

What if hell is ash and ribbon
corny songs sung badly
hangnails on every finger
endless canker sores
and only salt to eat?

What if hell is a dead cat
on your porch?

What if hell is sorrow
borne in your blood
an itch impossible
to scratch
and all that remains
of your story?

Decrepit

Nor are they unkind
these young
who see my white beard
and offer to carry my burdens
nor are they thoughtless
and cheaper meals
and movie discounts
are no insult
I have become Mr. Leo
to the beautiful flowers
who twist and stretch my limbs
with hands that might
have once demanded
sweeter things
and I suppose
physical therapy
is its own reward
but Mr. Leo is ancient
and is the name
the pretty young girls
called my father
when he became old
and anyway
my name is Jeff

Always

Quiet people
in dark hallways
a few of them
listening to the night

brave dandelions
straining through
sidewalk cracks

old men and dogs
dreaming
after their fashion
of bones

every mortal thing
falling in slow motion
beneath a sad
and flyaway moon

In the End

Everything fell from the statue
and crawled toward the city
toward the people drinking coffee
or wandering aimless streets
the people arguing
and the people asleep on benches
and some saw it coming
and thought they could fix things or hide
maybe escape
but there was nowhere to go
and the things crawling from the statue
came to the city
and the people were consumed for a time
and then some of them
went about their business
and some retreated to darkness
and when the bombs finally dropped
it was the children
who went to the statue
and stood there accusing the lie
and when death came
it came for everyone
and all that was left
was the statue
broken and burning
and then there was nothing
and no way home ever again

No Heart Known or Needed

Naked in hell
and the burning days
the trees dripping snakes

your feet
punctured by thorns

this game might fool some
but I know your favors

cast your spells
in the mystery tongue
adorned in juniper oil
red silk, linen, holly, ash

I come to you
on my dead breath
filled with dust
ragged and beaten to a stain
naked in hell
dripping snakes
needful
and burning

Please Pay Attention

You will never get all the stars out,
no matter how hard you try.

Most of them are unknown to you
and unrecognizable.

Perhaps, in some unexplored nook,
there is a hidden talent for the oboe,
or the wind dance of a forgotten Amazonian people.

Maybe, if you knew where to search,
you could manifest the precise inflection and cadence
to soothe a Russian boy whose mother has been taken by disease.

Maybe you have an unrealized knack for drawing fairies in colored sand.

The stars are in there,
in your brain and heart and skin,
and some of them you know,
like maybe you're good at baking,
or working crossword puzzles,
or writing a poem.

Maybe you paint portraits that hang on museum walls,
or write symphonies to make strong men weep,
or you are a tender and electrifying lover.

Maybe you uplift the masses.
Maybe you teach like a wizard.

Maybe you can beat any man
who steps in the ring.
Maybe you sculpt,
or write histories of the forgotten.

Maybe.
Maybe.
Maybe.

It doesn't matter.

There is so much more you could do.
So many other things you could give the world.

And if you were wondering
when you should start writing that novel,
please understand we each have a short clock
and it ticks like a bastard.

Do it now.

Do what you can and then do more.

The stars burn inside for a while,
delicious as the love who would not have you,
and then burn out.

And there is nothing worse
than the pain of dead stars
pulling you toward the grave.

This will happen no matter what you do,
but you can ease the pain a little.

Start now.

The stars are waiting,
and they have no sympathy for your weakness.

What Love Does

like joints gone
round the bend
and horrid bodies
that at their best
were never beautiful
children who disappoint
and someday
standing by a grave
with no hand in yours
waiting

Little Man

And your children's children's children
will become quaint relics
to the children of their distant babes
and you will be a smudged footnote
in a lost book
and all of today's headlines
will be dust forced on the bored young
who want only to love and fly
and get wasted in graveyards
like you did when life was fresh
trying to loose the grip of the stupid old
who did not understand the universe
had worked since time began
to bring you to exist
as the pinnacle of all things

The Death We Deserve

In the end was silence,
the word being spent in blood.
The streets flowed with the sons
and daughters of avarice
and a plague was upon the land.
Revenge became the currency
of the people
and was, by day and night,
spent with fury.
And in the dark corners
there arose a fire
of the wicked
who would hasten
the end of things
in the Lord's name.
And so it was done.
And a babe came unto the world
and the people said,
"Is this not the one
foretold by the prophets?
The one spoken of
by men of renown?"
And the babe was still and cold,
a dead and corrupted thing.
And all who saw, saw that it was good.
And a darkness was upon the land,
even until the end of days
and none remained to weep.

TWO

#NeverAgain

I am with you
as winds gather
as clouds pass untouched
as children dream big dreams
I am with you
as you drink your morning coffee
and hope for a better day
I am with you as graves multiply
as America awakens
as we finally understand
too much has happened
to go back to sleep
as we clasp hands
and embrace rage
as we stand
fierce
I am with you
as whatever is to come
begins

What We Allow

Wolves hunt
our children
and snakes wait
under the bed
angry cowards
have all the guns
they need
and every
good dream
is lined up
for slaughter

This Is What You Do

Keep it close
to the bone, boy.
Keep the blade busy.
You were never
going to be their darling
so what have you got to lose?
The body in your basement
is your own
and the blade stays sharp
if you use it right.
Serve up the blessed flesh.
They won't know
they're hungry
if you don't prepare
the feast.

Charlottesville

another deep cut
the body
can barely sustain

a day will come
when the blood tides break

when the fires
catch wind

and all refuge is consumed
as flame must always consume

as comfort becomes memory

as our children
cannot imagine peace

it is so simple
so easy to miss

Therefore

try to make the world better
but in small ways
people disagree
and grand visions
often end poorly
so deal in kindness
and listen to other people's troubles
pet your cat even when she does not insist
buy art from unknown genius
share bread and water
hold hands with the aged
and reveal love as it manifests
play with your children
and teach them courage
but also let them cry
there are stars inside you
and these are the stars
for which the world is waiting
that is the gift you bring
it is why you are here

American Dream

Enter Bonnie and Clyde
stage left

or Baby Face Nelson
maybe Pretty Boy Floyd

and stolen roadsters
racing thug cops
under crisp afternoon
October skies

every one of us ready
to be riddled with bullets
everyone here for victory

and Tommy guns blasting
pretty outlaws
and point blank refusal

West Texas sounds better
than you might think

and we'll maybe
make Arkansas by dawn
if we keep our nerve

drive on, cowboy
sweat is all you need
and white-knuckled grit

like diamonds
adorning the air

to stay alive tonight

Yesterday in Heaven

Yesterday in heaven
Billy Jack
and Bruce Lee
ripped on equal parts
peyote and Wild Turkey
were already
mad because
that tramp
Jayne Mansfield
played them
like high school punks
at an after-prom orgy
and ended up fucking
Bobby Darren anyway
and flipping them off
and laughing about it
so they were both
itching for a fight.

Well, yesterday
in Heaven
Billy Jack and Bruce Lee
those goofy bastards
fucked up like they were
they went on such a spree
beating the immortal shit
out of one another
and generally wrecking
the joint

'til Jesus put the hammer down
and knocked their heads together
and sent them right back to Earth
'til they could cool off some.

Shit.

Those motherfuckers
those bad men
are new babies now

and you new mommies
and you new daddies
better watch your ass.

Jesus is looking out for them
of course.
They're his boys
and he won't let them
mess up big time.
Or if he does, fuck it.
they can still go back home
when the time comes.

Sometimes heaven
even with Jayne Mansfield
on the prowl
can just fucking wait.
Jesus might just hit
that Himself.
Might do it
just to pass the time of day.

America Was Great, I Guess, When

Back when genuine cool
could still be a Coke
and a pair of Levi's
and no one knew
how the world would turn ash
back in those days
when long walks at night
were better
than just about anything
back when most of it worked
and we could pretend
the broken parts didn't matter
back when we were allowed
to ignore the hunger
that could not fill
because it belonged
to the others
back when we slept
inside a selfish dream
and never wanted
to awaken

MAGA

Listen, I eat nails for breakfast
and keep mountain lions for pets
since tigers are hard to find
and a hair too prissy.

I can whip any three men in a fair fight
and five if I hit low.
My heart is as hard as coal, and blacker,
and I can't begin to remember
how many women whose love
I've used and cast aside.

I'm meaner than Genghis Kahn
and twice as ugly.
I can't decide if I should fuck your mother next
or your daughter
but I can tell you your wife
is a decent lay,
even if she can't suck dick for shit.
I'll be at your place later on,
just to kick your ass for fun.

You know me, brother.
Don't act like you don't.

Listen now.
Hey, where do you think you're going?
Did I say you could leave?

Okay.
All right.
I see what's going on.

Forget it.
Forget that stuff.
Dumb shit can't take a joke.

Hey, put that down.
For God's sake stop hitting me.
Sweet Jesus. Stop.

Can't we just make America great again?

Evangelical

the churches are filled
with prayers and pot luck dinners
and people who love children
as long as their skin is white

the churches are filled
with joy and choir music
and the churches are filled
with frightened people
who do not understand this world
but hate it anyway

the churches
rally around the flag

the churches
are dragging us all into Hell
and the churches
know only English prayers
are answered
and never for the poor

Oh, Beautiful

Every man a king
and free behind
shuttered windows
patriots all and itching
to shoot black boys
or carve them up for sex
the promise of hot blood
on angry dicks
and every man a king in his red hat
with good people on both sides
and every man with his guns
and sexy redhead Russian fantasy
and every man mouthing slogans
and the walls closing in
and every man a king
in this land of gutted promise
bled dreams
and terrified punks
shaking fists at children
strutting like mad
seeing their destruction
coming hard
brown and angry
on every corner

Ain't that America?

Here's what you do:
First, don't be queer or colored
and if you're a woman
just shut the hell up and smile.

Them liberals come from Satan
to take your guns
and make you pray
to ramalamadingdong
or some shit.

Just do like I say.

If you don't do nothing wrong
the police ain't gonna fuck with you.

Comply, mother fucker.

Jesus Christ, boy.
It's all so fucking simple.

When are you people
gonna quit living in the past?

Twilight of Empire

someone has to say it
so let me start:

we are finished
it's over

no more complaining
no fretting over details
you couldn't control if you tried
and you are miles past trying

the streets are filled with faces
the streets are filled with blank stares
and rage

they are home to our shared tragedy
and we are too numb to understand

we look everywhere and see the enemy
we look and see the attributes
we are told to hate

every hand could grasp another's hand
every face could turn toward another face

the man at the gas station hates you
because you make too much money
or not enough
and someone on his television
says he should

the woman in the grocery store
has been warned about you
by her preacher

even your children are caged,
their minds pummeled by falsehoods
tarted up like fun

soon, they will hate you too

the world is not working

people roam the lonely streets
searching for a leader
they want to hear that they are correct
to hate, justified in their fear

they want to know it is okay
to think of killing

some want to kill blacks,
some believe whites must be eliminated
with others, it is police
or politicians of a particular party
or those who might vote for them

I'm certain there are those
who have it in for Koreans
or people from Peru or Canada

and everyone hates Muslims, right?

your barber hates Mexicans
the pretty checkout girl
at the pharmacy hates gays

the people in your church
hate the people in the church
down the street
and don't think a whole lot of you

we live inside a game
held fast by a riddle

follow the lies
follow the money
follow the power

follow everyone who makes you
want to hate
and you will be lost in the maze

these are tricks, friend
follow them down the rabbit hole
and still you will be wrong

the unseen hand is at your throat
the unseen hand is jacking you off
the unseen hand can be a fist or a flower

I am finished
I am over it

the days are the same days
whether you suck down the fairy tale or not,
and I am through with the poison

so long

What We Now Endure

The people have always been mad
but afraid to show it

or maybe they were unsure what their madness was
until someone came along
to give it a name.

The people sat in their homes and worried.

Husbands tormented wives
while wives made sure their husbands lived in hell
and children were taught that this is the way of things.

The people have been mad forever
and their madness drives all sorrow.

It screams inside their heads
that someone is coming to kill them
or take away their blessings.

It whispers to them on dark nights
of all the horrors their neighbors are surely doing.

It leaves small threatening notes on their dressers
or in the pockets of their clothing.

The madness begs for a leader,
demands it.

The madness craves direction
because it is fear
and fear is a confused child punching walls.

Make no mistake:
It is a killing madness.

Maybe it kills you,
maybe me;
maybe it only kills the mad.
Most likely it kills the weak and innocent
because the mad hate these people most of all.

And their rage is righteous and pure

It is flame and hammers.
It is reptilian and poison.
It is wasps in the brain.

It is all the hurt they have endured
and no capacity to understand.

And their rage knows no limit.

And no one
no one
will stand in their way
when they come for you.

We have seen this before.
Remember?

Holy Hell

It's fine to avoid
eye contact;

they expect it
and most everyone does.

Only fools give handouts
and the stench is revolting.

Even knowing they're
on the streets
turns my stomach.

It's not my fault
if they have children,
and feeding them now
only makes for
stronger thugs later.

Don't get me started
on paying for their health care.

And don't get me wrong,

I give to lots of charities
through the church
and it all goes
to the deserving.

God's work ain't cheap, brother.
Let us pray.

Just Saying

Your God is an asshole.
It's the only explanation.
I mean, we know you're
a good person, right?
I see how you want us
all to get along.
You even want to get along
with the horrible liberals.
I know you do.
If only they would just
come around and
stop being so mean.
I know you're a good person
and you were raised right.
God and country all the way.
So I know you wouldn't want
children going hungry
or people sleeping
in the streets
or dying because
they have no health care
or being abused
because of their religion
or who they love.
I know you don't want women
treated as objects
molested
subjugated.
What kind of good person
would want any of this?

Not you, of course.
Never you.
So it must be that asshole God
you rave about.
It must be that asshole God
that wants these bad things.
It must be that asshole God,
the one you keep saying you fear.
That asshole God
is abusing you, right?
Making you do things
you don't like?
Making you hurt people?
Making you judge your neighbor
and laugh about it
as you plot their death?
What an asshole your God is.
Maybe the old God retired.
Maybe the old God died.
Maybe the old God
became an alcoholic
and is a really mean drunk.
The God you grew up with
was love, right?
And now you're stuck
with this asshole God
and you've got to obey.
Shit. That's awful.
I hope you can find a way out.
I really do.
The first step is admitting
there's a problem,
but you already see the problem,
don't you?

I mean, you're a good person, right?
I know you would never be an asshole on your own.
Right?

Revelation

It's like they say
in the Bible
or someplace
fire and water
gonna end it all
and that ol' Satan
be watching over
the end times
on his big TV
when he's not throwing
paper towels at people
dying of thirst
all them folks shot down
and we've already moved on
this world is a cobweb
being swept away
and that ol' Satan, he's smart
just ask him
and he's gonna let it all drown and burn
and, don't you know,
there ain't no one to blame
for him doing it
but us?

Beast

And on that day he went forth
and the world was aflame.
And the people hid amongst
the smoke and ash.
And he said to them
"Do not fear for I am with you."
And still the people hid and he said,
"I am your savior, the one for whom
you have voted. Come forth
and bring me worship."
And the people found strength
and came unto him
and a brave girl child spake.
"You are he, the one
who has ravaged our fields and cities
the one who has raped our mothers
and butchered our fathers
the one who has eaten all of our hearts.
You are he who has laid waste the Earth."
And he gave assent, saying,
"I am that I am.
I have done all that I said I would do
no more than that and no less.
This is the world we have made together."
And the girl child spake.
"You have destroyed those
who gave you power
and all that remains are
what you see, we children.

We few are the last of the people,
the last of our lines, the last of those
over whom you held sway,
the children who did not
vote for you, neither would we ever,
and we rebuke you."
And he said in terrible anger,
"I am your savior, the one chosen
by the Russian bear,
the one known through
all the world for my riches and towers
and television show.
I am vast in my world
and my world is all."
And the girl child spake.
"You are as a leech
and are also as the corrupt things
that crawl upon dung
and feed on blood and festering wounds
and we will not suffer you."
And she turned
and gathered the children about her
and bid them follow her to a new land.
But the world was aflame
and no land remained.
And the end of things was about them.
And the end came to him last of all.
And with the last breath he drew
he looked upon his works
and he smiled
and he saw that it was good.

Your Turn

It is not allowed
Step forward and prepare
Believe the central message
Crime is death
It is not allowed
Step forward and prepare
Your duty is silence
Believe the central message
Your duty is to the one
And the one is not you
It is not allowed
Step forward and prepare
It is time for sacrifice
Time for your duty
Time to deny all flesh
To blind yourself to horror
To believe the central message
Step forward and prepare
You may close your eyes if you like
The next one is waiting

The American Way

Citizen relent
You impede our progress
Citizen relent
You endanger the republic
Citizen relent
You put yourself at risk
Citizen relent
You nurture those who are not like us
Citizen relent
You disregard the plan
Citizen relent
You are not American
as I am American
Citizen relent
I will not tell you again

You Know there Are Places Like That

small rooms with bare shelves
pantries empty of food
and refrigerators used for
a bit of milk or stale bologna
rooms for old men or ancient women
the light gone
the light that was once there gone
starved into its own apocalypse
fallen onto its knees
ravaged

or houses with mothers or fathers
who can't feed their children
houses where day-old bread is a luxury
and tomorrow will be the same

you know there are places like that
you have read about them in books
you have seen them in movies
and afterward you have gone
for a bite to eat

or off to discuss the finer points
of the story
with your intelligent friends

or home to snug comfort

you know there are places like that
and worse places still
and you might make words which say
you are saddened by this

but the truth is you are happy
and safe and warm
and you don't really care
don't really give a damn
about these places
or the people
who are trapped within

this will kill your soul
if you have any soul
left to kill

you know there are places like that
you know there are women
and children and men
starving

and you do nothing
and someday you will die
and you will not be missed
so live it up

and sweet dreams
I guess

May 4

My daughter stomps
on the bubble wrap
from the box my books came in
and it is loud, like gunshots.
My son doesn't like the noise
and neither do I
but I let her do it
because it makes her happy
and it's over so fast we can forget
and move on.
We're running late anyway
in a rush to get in the car
and when we are safely
inside and moving
I ask them if they know
why May 4 is important.
They do not
so I ask
if they have heard of
Kent State
and they have not,
so I tell them of the war in Vietnam
and the protests across America
and the one in Ohio
that drew the national guard
to a college campus
and the shots that rang out
and the four students killed.
My children don't say anything
so I say they need to remember

Kent State
so maybe it won't happen again.
My son says that it will happen
and he seems sure of it
but calm
and soon I'm dropping him off
at his high school
and then my daughter
at her elementary school
where active shooter drills
are common enough to be boring
and angry young men everywhere
keep guns at the ready
for their special purpose
on a day maybe determined
but not yet revealed
as the birds sing
and the sun shines
and the world goes around
and around and around
like it does
with nothing new to say

Quiet Jim

Jim was filled with hate and Jesus
and loved all the guns he owned
and all the guns he thought
he might get sometime
and was scared crazy by queer shadows
and all those Mexicans come to rape
and tear down statues
of the honored confederate dead.

Jim knew learning is for suckers
and kids could be so mean
so somebody might as well
shoot up the schools
and, anyway, dead children
make happy martyrs for the libtards.

Jim hummed tunelessly
as he marched
toward the place
where no one
had been willing
to love him
as his mantra played
over and over in his head:

"We forgive nothing.
We forgive nothing.
We forgive nothing."

Life, he was pretty sure,
is what you make it.
Today, Jim would be a king.

Something You Should Know

the snakes in your house
hide better than children
the snakes hide in your bed
flattened against the sheets
so you don't even know
they are there
they hide in the milk
and the cupboards
the snakes hate your routine
but work around it
the snakes eat your ice cream sandwiches
and crawl on you as you sleep
they work with the spiders and rats
and the dirty dishes in your dirty sink
they work with the shit in your toilet
and the shit in your head
the snakes only want to love you
after their snaky fashion
and you can't figure out
what that means
the snakes wait for the right moment
and that could be never
and it is possible they will not strike
will not crush you
but either way
there is nothing
to be done
the snakes aren't going anywhere
and neither
dear one
are you

Believe It

as the dark flanks us
as the light shudders
there is a place
for fierce shields
against the iron fist
in the barbwire glove
a place to lift the weary and spent
to embrace the resurrected Juden
held up as threat and denied
the falsely accused
the scapegoats
the easy targets
there is a place
for truth declaimed with righteous fury
and written on the houses of the rich
inscribed in the halls of power
etched into the fabric of our days
there is a place even for poems
and we live together in that place
or die silent and alone
a place for art
right here
right now
it's as easy as breathing
and as hard

In Dubious Battle

The front lines
are exhausting
but that's not news
there isn't time
for what needs
to happen
everyone is angry
or else devastated
tears are common
and we are not surprised
to be against this wall
and somebody
has a trigger to pull
and the waiting
will destroy us all

In Our Time

The streets are quiet
as night falls
and stars twinkle
and it is cold
and beautiful faces
on television
convey the death
of America
and the shopping malls are busy
and the churches are filled
with good Christians
who love the psychopath
they put in the White House
and the radio plays forgettable music
and the Super Bowl is coming up
and young lovers love
and it is quiet for now
and perhaps our death
will be easy
so easy we don't even know
but maybe
just maybe
America is about
to explode

New Testament

Eighteen years past the millennium
and I search for signs.
Elvis is still dead, but Donald Trump lives.
There are floods and hurricanes and fires
and strange, awful deaths.
Mothers drowning children.
Cannibalism.
Schools riddled with bullets.
Will there be a star in the east?
And will astronomers tell us
it is only sunspot activity
or Venus doing handstands?
And will we listen? And to whom?
And will any sane person have hope?
And will the people gather
at the gates of Graceland
and stare through the bars?
And will they see the sign?

One Who Came Before

Sappho addressed Aphrodite
like a sister,
had handsome brothers
and a daughter, Kleis,
more beautiful than the flowers.
She wrote of a country girl
who bewitched Andromeda,
her rival, without even the sense
to raise her ragged dress
and show her legs,
a country girl,
dead for twenty-five centuries,
still lovely this second.
Sappho, short, dark and ugly,
orphaned young,
most of her work long lost,
believed she would be
remembered
in another time,
and here we are.
If that doesn't get you
through the night,
what will?

Naps Are the Best

Dozing on the couch
with the TV muted
as the news reports
an alien invasion
and the coincidence
of monsters by the legion
crawling from lakes
and the undead clawing
from their graves
dozing on the couch
as the talking heads shriek
about nuclear missiles
slamming into
national monuments
and vengeful wizards
calling demons to feast
on entrails and children
dozing in delicious oblivion
with the TV muted
and your street still quiet
and sweet dreams
holding you close
for one second more

This Is the Truth

Each person
is a mystery poet
but we mostly
choose slumber.
Cats and starlight
try to nudge us awake
but we sleep so well
even through our
hurricane dreams.

The Circle Is Not Jealous of the Sphere
But that Doesn't Mean
They Will Take Tea on a Summer Day

Imagine an immense golden sphere, so big that its boundaries mesh exactly with the boundaries of the multiverse. The sphere is perfect and gleaming and it will exist as long as you watch it. You notice the sphere is spinning. Your fascination will not let you look away. Now, imagine that this sphere is composed of a vast number of layers of diminishing size down to the smallest possible sphere at the center and each made of a different state of matter and spinning at an angle to the one below it. The angles are so small as not to be detectable by any means but there are enough layers that all possible angles are contained in all possible directions with each sphere in each possible state of matter. The outer sphere, the one you see, is precisely large enough to contain this. The internal spheres are composed of every existing or potential state of matter for each angle at every possible rate of spin. Each will randomly change velocity and direction at irregular intervals until all possible combinations of speed, angle, direction and state of matter have occurred and for all possible lengths of time with relation of each sphere to every other. Imagine that spinning multitude bisected to describe every possible circle it contains, moment by moment, until every possible bisection has occurred with the spinning spheres in every possible point of rotation in relation to every other sphere and the kinetic and potential energy it describes. You will remain focused on the outer sphere until all of this is complete at which point you will lose interest and look away. What is the sum of motion? What is implied? What will happen when everything stops? What will happen when you look away?

ONE

Prophesy Some

Can you name
when you took
the great horned Jesus
with piercing fingers and fire?
Can you name when you took
the tongue and eyes of dust?
Tell me the moment when, please.
Tell me the hour of return.
Can you tell the road back
to the Spanish moss
in the suffocating trees?
Can you find me the way?
You weary, fiendish slut of yesterday.
We are glory. Roll down the windows. Drive.

We don't stop while we're breathing.

My Baby Wrote Me a Letter

"Why do these crazy people
keep following me around?
I haven't done anything wrong,"
she said, telling me then about
Gerald Ford on TV taking the swine flu vaccine
just so SHE would take it
and why would the President do that to HER?
Okay, this was a while back,
but I wonder sometimes what became of her
with her red hair and freckles
and strange, sad eyes
and nobody following her around
crazy or not.

Annelise Sometime

Sitting in a car
with a red-headed girl
drinking Cuban rum
from the bottle
or swimming with her
in a cold lake
in just underwear
stuck to your body and hers
like new skin
late-night phone calls
whispered surrender
everything you ever wanted
dreams dreams dreams

The Deadliest Man Alive

I wanted Telecult Power
and voodoo
Count Dante's secrets

I wanted to be the world's
most dangerous something
though I would of course
use my powers for good

I wanted to be the one
kicking sand in some guy's face
if there was going to be any sand kicked

I wanted flying saucers overhead
and landing in the empty lot
down the street

Charles Atlas and dynamic tension
seemed an answer
to questions I didn't know to ask
and masked ninja masters called to me

I definitely did not want
to make extra cash selling flower seeds
and I never considered
learning guitar by mail
or looking suave with a false beard

though I really did want to send off
for a pet monkey

but my parents said no

so I ordered sea monkeys
and I got x-ray specs
and vampire blood
and a life size poster
of a moon monster

the submarine big enough
to get inside and fire torpedoes
never came
even though I sent a check
from my very own bank account

and those days are gone
and most everyone I loved is dead
or might as well be
and they haven't made
a good comic book
in forty years

When We Left that Day

Flowers swayed
in their red battalions
and the sky bloomed
into thunderclouds
as ragged, half-grown children
sang their lovely songs.

Mary said it was a wonder
and hugged me tight
as snakes hung
from long branches
and our river reversed its course.

You could smell smoke for miles
and everything was consumed.

Flame took the world
in its coquettish way and,
like Mary and I in our splendor,
danced a hungry waltz,
licking the soft throat
of the blood-red sky.

Sanctuaries

together
in small rooms
or streets
light breaking
in waves
the shape
of your face
in my hands
two people
outside time
turned now
to confetti
and given
to the wind

Caught

That time you
were frozen in place
with the violins playing
maybe there was rain
and it was near dark
someone's breath
on your chest
that time the music
took you
and the rhythm of breath
and hands on your skin
you couldn't even think
of names

Something Like Love

He stood in the rain
in his black fedora
hard leather shoes
tapping puddles.

She drew the curtain
and put on tea
while shadows fell
and the rain came hard
all that day and night.

He wondered on love
by the tick of the clock
while she dreamed of roses
and slept on silk
as he stood in his shoes in the rain.

Sweet Life

"Life ain't no bucket of honey,"
she said, dropping her silken gown.
"More like, it's a goblet of bees."

"Hush now, Madge," said Henry,
"and let me love you."

"You are a fool," she sighed.
"A damned, bloody fool."

Madge paused, eyes wet and blinking.
"Well, come on, then."

Tomorrow came soon enough,
as did the bees.

Red Flowers

she said we are all
haunted by roses
not received
and roses rejected
and by those not offered
most of all
she said this in the dark
and from across the room
in a small house
so far from my home
as we drowned in roses
crimson and fragrant
but gone

Repitition of Saturday Night

Someone always
gets their heart broken

and smoke
from a crushed cigarette
decorates the air
above a crystal ashtray

there are drinks involved
usually whiskey

and we cannot forget
the silence
that stakes home
in the shocked blood

blonde hair and blue eyes
a tight dress just so

a particular voice
that was alive
in the moments
that mattered

Eternal

Father and son
in their small green car
driving in the rain
to the son's school
and there is mostly silence.
The father wants to tell the son
that the son is like him
or worse
that he is like the son.
But the son is 14
and the father is old
and since they are indeed alike
he knows his son
will not welcome the observation.
When they arrive
the father stops the car
and the son gets out
and the father
watches him
walk away.
The father says
a little too loudly
"Have fun and learn a lot"
and the son turns a quarter
and nods once
up then down
and they both head,
unhappily,
to the places
they are required to go.

These Are the Things We Cannot Bear

Deloris left her mark on him so easy,
the way drowning is easy
when all that remains
is the decision to breathe.
He stayed in his room for a week
after she left,
a carton of smokes
and two fifths of bourbon,
that was all he needed.
Deloris was four states over
when he hung himself in the bathroom
with the necktie he wore that first night,
the night they went dancing at the Palace,
and she never even heard about it.
Not much later,
she was in love with a butcher
she met in a five and dime.
This time it was for real.
She was sure of it.
After all, broken hearts
only happen to the beautiful.

Hello, It's Me

Would this world be easier to bear
if you knew you have loved
and lost and loved again
everyone you will ever meet
in this tawdry life
through age upon uncounted age
and that even I, grotesque,
was once your heart's sharp prize?

Buttercup and T-Bone

We were going to travel the country
visiting Wal-Marts
and write a book about it.

The plan was to get a motorcycle
with a sidecar
and I would call you Buttercup
and you would call me T-Bone.

We would write a coffee table book,
maybe, with a bunch of photographs.

The idea was that no matter
where we were,
it could be anywhere,
and the Wal-Mart in Kalamazoo
would be identical
to the Wal-Mart in Knoxville
or any other place
but still be its own thing.

You have to remember
that we drank a lot in those days,
but it seemed like a good idea
at the time,

and I still swear by it,
just as I did
when we made our secret plans,
all giddy and in love
this dream of the road with you.

On Any Quiet Street

strange child
picks up a dying
butterfly and
begs it to live
pets and prays
and rides off
on a blue bicycle
the day like any other
bound up in the mystery:
for a moment he is flying

Those Were the Days

Thirty years old
and rolling down a hill
right into the street
the old lady
stopped her car
an inch from my head
I should have
quit drinking
then and there
but I climbed
back up the hill
had another beer
and rolled
right down
again

Heartbeat

Still a child at 30
unashamed and shuffling
down the sidewalk
with joy like I might explode
drunk most of the time
or devouring books
like steak and candy
in hopeless love
with one who never
loved me back
and writing my poems
as free as anyone ever was
as I ever would be
and I tell you now
I'm still there
my feet echo on that pavement
and nothing ever dies
if you don't let it

Nighthawks

The buzzing is whispers broken now and then
by shrieks of laughter making the room glow hot

as back in the kitchen Mary runs damp fingers
through dishwater blonde
and takes a long drag on that last cigarette

two hours 'til closing
and her corns acting up
a quick glance in the mirror

forcing a smile, she steps into the arena
forgetting impotent prayers
wading through the come-ons and sly glances

noticing the hand gliding past the knee
at table five, up toward the waiting crotch:

a prize for the woman to slap and scold
so everyone will know his desire

again the shrieks, laughter bouncing
from blind walls, dying quickly
after making its brave assertions

Mary takes her pad to five and awaits her orders
her eyes fixed to the hair on the back of his hands

she waits as they insinuate their reply

while above, the fluorescent lights hum
and beat back the darkness

Reading *Pomes All Sizes*
Outdoors at Ole Miss, Oct., 1992

Grooving on Kerouac
while a bird slips
from blue sky to
yellow green leaves
head back light
on untender majesty
of concrete column
watching sweetbutter
girlies float and flitter
feeling good in my balls
like Jack and everybody

Prestonsburg and All of It

It is a tumbled land
of coal and hollows
scrub pine, maples
the orange and red
mountains of October
this place where I first loved
and was loved back
and all the pretty girls
of yesterday
are grandmothers
or old enough to be
and of course still beautiful
this land of fox and copperhead
murky rivers and winter snow
sometimes deep to the knees
and there was that time
the Big Sandy froze solid
and Phil Bishop and I
walked right across it
neither of us letting on
we were scared
and that December
we built an igloo in my yard
big enough to stand in
and it lasted through February
this homeplace of ghosts of good dogs
and friends like the blood
of the best summer of your life
with the days tumbling
down secret hillsides

in a race with shadows
and always, like our hearts in love,
picking up speed

Fun in the Sun

Waking hungover
beneath a hedge
in Key West
is better
than it sounds
waking in a hedge
is fine
even if you're lost
and the girl is gone
waking in a hedge
after searching
all night
waking in a hedge
as the pelicans fly
and the indifferent sun
beats you down
and happy people
wander bright streets
waking in a hedge
before you find her
and everything
falls into place
for just an hour
waking in a hedge
while you are
alive and raging
stupid as a fish
and young enough
to matter

Floyd County

It begins in the sandstone caves,
the caves where you went as a boy,
to hide and look out over the mountains.
You called them the Three Story Caves,
and they only went back a little way into the hill,
small pockets of dim stillness.
From Lookout Point you could see
Ball Alley Curve five hundred feet down
and the Big Sandy, a brown snake sleeping.
There was a swinging bridge.
You could hear the cars on 23 if you strained,
but it was the wind blowing through the trees
that you listened to.
The sun was hot.
It was that kind of day: green and living.
It begins in these caves on a day like this
and runs and runs across hollows and secrets
and wildflowers, among strip mines and snakes,
with every old dog you've ever owned,
and the shy, pretty girls you have kissed and longed for.
And it runs to the highways leading someplace else,
to other dim, still pockets, and to places you cannot know,
not even after years within them,
to cities and faraway states and land that is flat with the earth.
This place is its own small miracle.
There are always beginnings and if the caves belong to you,
they belong to the world.
Here is the magic:
You are still there, even now. This has always been true,
even when you did not see it.
Even when you did not understand.

About the Author

Jeff Weddle grew up in Prestonsburg, a small town in the hill country of Eastern Kentucky. He has worked as a public library director, disc jockey, newspaper reporter, Tae Kwon Do teacher, and fry cook, among other things. His first book, *Bohemian New Orleans: The Story of the Outsider and Loujon Press* (University Press of Mississippi, 2007), won the Eudora Welty Prize and helped inspire Wayne Ewing's documentary, *The Outsiders of New Orleans: Loujon Press* (Wayne Ewing Films, 2007). He teaches in the School of Library and Information Studies at the University of Alabama.

Grateful Acknowledgement is made to the following, where some of these poems previously appeared, sometimes in slightly different form:

Alien Buddha Press, The Alien Buddha Wears a Yellow Vest, Beau Blue Presents: American Minutes, Betray the Invisible, Blue's Cruzio Café, Bouillabaisse, Gypsy Art Show, Hello Poetry, Journal of Kentucky Studies, Kentucky Writing, Morehead Poets, Old Red Kimono, Pressure Press Presents, Rust Belt Press, Unlikely Stories Mark V, and *Wingnut Brigade.*

Other Titles by Jeff Weddle

A Puncher's Chance (Rust Belt Press, 2019)

It's Colder than Hell / Starving Elves Eat Reindeer Meat / Santa Claus is Dead (Alien Buddha Press, 2018)

Heart of the Broken World (Nixes Mate Books, 2017)

Comes to This (Nixes Mate Books, 2017)

When Giraffes Flew (Southern Yellow Pine Publishing, 2015)

The Librarians's Guide to Negotiation: Winning Strategies for the Digital Age (co-author, Information Today, Inc., 2012)

Betray the Invisible (OEOCO, 2010)

Bohemian New Orleans: The Story of the Outsider and Loujon Press (University Press of Mississippi, 2007)

Recent Titles from Unlikely Books

The Mercy of Traffic by Wendy Taylor Carlisle

Cantos Poesia by David E. Matthews

Left Hand Dharma: New and Selected Poems by Belinda Subraman

Apocalyptics by C. Derick Varn

Pachuco Skull with Sombrero: Los Angeles, 1970 by Lawrence Welsh

Monolith by Anne McMillen (Second Edition)

When Red Blood Cells Leak by Anne McMillen (Second Edition)

My Hands Were Clean by Tom Bradley (Second Edition)

anonymous gun. by Kurtice Kucheman (Second Edition)

Soy solo palabras but wish to be a city by Leon De la Rósa, illustrated by Gui.ra.ga7 (Second Edition)

Blue Rooms, Black Holes, White Lights by Belinda Subraman (Second Edition)

Scorpions by Joel Chace

Ghazals 1-59 and Other Poems by Sheila E. Murphy and Michelle Greenblatt

brain : storm by Michelle Greenblatt (Second Edition, originally anabasis Press)

My Hands Were Clean by Tom Bradley (Second Edition)

Definitions of Obscurity by Vernon Frazer and Michelle Greenblatt (Second Edition of *Dark Hope*, Argotist E-Books)

ANCHOR WHAT by Vernon Frazer

ASHES AND SEEDS by Michelle Greenblatt

Love and Other Lethal Things by K. R. Copeland

52732993R00071

Made in the USA
Lexington, KY
19 September 2019